The Holy Bible Capsulated into One Sermon: A Paradigm in 66 Pages by Michael Dean Sweetser Ph.D. Pastoral Theology.

MICHAEL DEAN SWEETSER

authorHOUSE®

AuthorHouse™
1663 Liberty Drive
Bloomington, IN 47403
www.authorhouse.com
Phone: 1-800-839-8640

Published by AuthorHouse   11/12/2015

ISBN: 978-1-4969-5487-9 (sc)
ISBN: 978-1-4969-5486-2 (e)

CONTENTS

PREFACE

Polytechnic honor graduate qualifications of the author: Michael Dean Sweetser, Ph.D. pastoral theology.

United States Army, Military OSUT Academy Honor Graduate, 3/7th unit, Fort Sill, Oklahoma 1986.

United States Army, 25th Infantry Division Commanding General's Physical Fitness Award and presidential recognition of a challenge, promise, delivery resurrection world record from a "brain dead timetable" Oahu, Hawaii 1988.

United States Army Meritorious Citation, Army Achievement Medal, Good Conduct Medal, Lightfighter Certification's I, II. Weapons expert: M-16, grenade, .45, M-60, 50 Cal., 105mm., 155mm. 3/7th & 1/8th units, 1986-Schofield Barracks, Hawaii 1989.

Law Enforcement Correctional Academy Honor Graduate for "Leadership" and 4.0 GPA. Weapons expert: .357 mag., Police Shotgun. Evergreen College, San Jose, California 1990.

United States Army, Honorable Discharge 1994.

Assemblies of God License to Preach clergy credential, national exam rated: 4.0 GPA. Global University, Springfield, Missouri 2002.

Senior pastor of Celeste Villa Church. 2001-Modesto, California 2003.

Correctional police chief letter for Honorable Tenure, evidenced by 7 letters of commendation with a 3 year E.R.T. certification, and 14 year competent rating, Santa Clara County Department of Correction 2003.

Republican Congressional Committee's published recognition in the "Wall Street Journal" of Michael Sweetser's influential leadership of business ethics 2003.

Republican National Committee's Eisenhower Commission, endorsed by three United States president's for "Integrity," who witnessed my world record on October 12, 1988. Also included was a letter of intent for Michael Sweetser's name to be engraved on the Ronald Reagan Memorial in Washington D.C. 2006.

Doctor of Philosophy, Pastoral Theology. 3.85 GPA equivalent for dissertation manuscripts synthesized duality version of the spiritual theology infusion transposition as God's personified minister revenger for a Master of Science, Criminal Justice 2011.

SUBJECT: THE HOLY BIBLE CAPSULATED INTO ONE SERMON: A PARADIGM IN 66 PAGES

Theme: Investigating conscience, wrath, & blessing.

Preponderant proposition: The tripartite reality, "Self examination" that can't blame anyone else for its own liabilities," 1 Corinthians 11:28-31.

"Can theology, man and organizational structures unilaterally maintain their individual integrity and still cope together to facilitate and present the highest ethical and moral standards of sociological order and good?"

SERMONIC INTRODUCTION

Part I:

We begin with the illumination of the providential evolution of the Law, within the Grace and Truth's covenant image, Romans 3:31, Acts 13:39, justified as holy, harmless, undefiled distinction from sinners, by willful and premeditated intellectual transposition, personifying a volitional reciprocating spiritual motive and intent, bodily manifested from intestinal fortified purpose and mission statement's total likeness, capsulating a preeminently postured understanding that the yeilded body, soul, spirit image sustains the infusion symbols of the mastery of the anointed imulation excellency revealing Father's delegated power through the Son's dignity of character traits, 1 Corinthians 1:24, empowered by that Holy Spirit for supernatural enhancement of intellect, gifts, talents, ability and sustainable strengthening marathon service, "to open their eyes, in order to turn them from darkness to light, and from the power of satan to God, that they may receive forgiveness of sins and an inheritance among those who are sanctified by faith in Me," Acts 26:18, to perpetuate a prognosticator likeness promoter of, "Self examination that can't blame anyone else for its own liabilities."

Part II:

Recently I paid a visit to my local department of motor vehicles and inquired about the cost to renew one of my vehicles registrations.

The vehicle I was inquiring about had been placed in a non-operational status due to some financial constraints I had experienced in the past, or at least that's the excuse I gave the D.M.V. attendant.

Over the course of a six month period, I had observed my vehicle remain in a non-op status. The vehicle was parked in the driveway in front of my home.

Day after day, week after week, month after month, the vehicle remained stationary in a stored position. The vehicle was never moved, appearing powerless, useless, and silently still eroding away. The stormy seasonal winds had distributed a film of dirt and decay causing a visibly disturbing smear to appear on the entire body. The once very capable, reliable, finely polished vehicle with extremely low mileage just sat silently and motionlessly, while every other empowered polished vehicle in the community continually passed by as though crying out, "follow me." The brakeshoes beyond the interior of the wheels base even began to become rusty.

Due to this very disturbing Revelation experience I had encountered, I decided to immediately make a clear and decisive choice. No longer would I allow the vehicle to remain idle and silently still. The vehicle really desired to be transformed and changed into an empowered, showroom driven vehicle, driven by an occupant able to expose darkness with its brillantly illuminating lamps. I realized that the occupant always desires to occupy the vehicle, however, the vehicle must be in a lawful, operational status to allow the occupant to effectively and efficiently steer the vehicle down an especially narrow road.

At this point, I applaud you if your spiritual discernment abilities have recognized the metaphor I have intended to effectively communicate to the understanding adherents, by a key principle, relating to a very powerful truth.

How many people today can honestly look themselves in the mirror and state without hesitation that they are a fully empowered driven Christian, thereby creating a fully empowered driven Church, driven by the Holy Spirit. How many people will agree that there are still powerless, uselessly stored vehicles that don't even make a sound, and eventually become stagnated and erode in their Christian existence.

The Holy Spirit desires to occupy and empower our vehicles for the benefit of the Kingdom of God right here in our present circumstances and even abroad. The Holy Spirit desires to occupy and empower our vehicles at a very high rate of acceleration. Remember, 1 Peter 4:7 declares: "The end of all things is at hand, therefore be serious and watchful in your prayers."

There clearly remains a certain urgency and expectancy in the atmosphere that we all breathe. We can no longer allow our vehicles to be driven by fear and doubt, but faith and obedience with the empowerment of the Holy Spirit to lead us out of the non-operational status quo that we so desperately need to remain apart from.

As we are nearing some sort of culmination of all things, let's not be Christians in a non-op status any longer. Let's be Christians who are restored, renewed, ready to accelerate, ready to sound our horns, and ready to be delivered to the throne-room for the sake of the Gospel and the Kingdom of God.

Part III:

Therefore, the imperative is extremely urgent for the creative potential to begin an introspective examination of the nucleus of spiritual motives and intents that ultimately and predominately posture the free-will agent's ability and capacity of body, soul and spirit, 1 Thessalonians 5:23, Hebrews 4:12; 10:22 to responsibly engage the sociological complexity of the economy of the world with a properly skilled and influentially talented, blamelessly irreproachable personification, derived from a psychologically constructed literary preeminence of a ceiling of righteousness world view, formulated from "a holy legal contract New Covenant standards package armorment" that requires transposition apprehension for rooted depth, through reciprocal consecration for living epistle citizenship attainment, comprehensively preserved from it's immutable kingdom coming sanctified perspectives of consecrated global vision for industrious purpose and mission; to ascertain the full benefits package of the spiritual and material promises, "according to the delegated theocratic instrument and provision of God's power that is autonomous congruence by proxy," 2 Corinthians 1:20, so that we are properly measuring the conscience by a transcending diagnostic reverberating from any repugnant ignominious disasters, thwarted for the integral blessing effects derived from the preeminently defined theological integrity integration of synthesizing the technical depth of competence, mastery and perfection's vicarious representation and presentation's exaltation by the postulating law of faith's parameters being actively exercised through the postulant's lifestyle and vocation that produces the "truth anointing," Isaiah 10:27, Ephesians 3:20; 4:1, 1 John 2:27.

OUTLINED SCRIPTURE TEXT

Our investigation of: "Conscience, wrath & blessing."

Prophecy, Isaiah 61:1-4 toward an approximate 700 year journey to Luke 4:17-21 Messianic fulfillments.

Mathematics: The science of numbers and of shapes in space quantified from: Empirical "quantum theorized" theological etymology that is exponentially eternal.

FATHER: 1) **OATH** **SANCTITY** **RICHES**	**"THE SPIRIT OF THE LIVING GOD IS UPON ME, BECAUSE HE HAS ANOINTED ME TO PREACH THE GOSPEL TO THE POOR, TO BIND UP THE BROKENHEARTED, TO PROCLAIM LIBERTY TO THE CAPTIVES, AND OPEN THE EYES OF THE BLIND,**
Algebra:	Branch of mathematics using symbols.
SON: 2) **LAW** **CHARACTER** **HONOR**	**TO OPEN PRISON DOORS TO THOSE WHO ARE BOUND, AND TO PROCLAIM THE ACCEPTABLE YEAR OF THE LORD AND THE DAY OF VENGEANCE OF OUR GOD. TO COMFORT ALL THAT MOURN,**
Geometry:	Mathematics of the relations, properties, and measurements of solids, surfaces, lines and angles.

HOLY SPIRIT: 3) **COVENANT** **NATURE** **LIFE**	**TO CONSOLE THOSE WHO MOURN IN ZION, TO BRING BEAUTY FOR ASHES AND THE OIL OF JOY FOR MOURNING, TO PUT ON THE GARMENTS OF PRAISE FOR THE SPIRIT OF HEAVINESS THAT THEY MIGHT BE CALLED TREES OF RIGHTEOUSNESS, THE PLANTING OF THE LORD, THAT HE MIGHT BE GLORIFIED,**
Trigonometry:	Mathematics dealing with triangular measurement.
TRIPARTITE: 4) **LOYALTY** **FREEWILL** **KINGDOM**	**THAT THEY MIGHT BUILD THE OLD WASTE, AND RAISE UP THE FORMER DESOLATIONS, AND THEY SHALL REPAIR THE WASTE CITIES, THE DESOLATIONS OF MANY GENERATIONS."**
Calculus:	Higher mathematics dealing with rates of change.

PREPONDERANT INTERROGATIVE PROPOSITION: THE TRIPARTITE REALITY, "SELF EXAMINATION THAT CAN'T BLAME ANYONE ELSE FOR IT'S OWN LIABILITIES." 1 CORINTHIANS 11:28-31.

THE QUESTION THEN ARISES FOR OUR EVALUATION: "CAN THEOLOGY, MAN AND ORGANIZATIONAL STRUCTURES' UNILATERALLY MAINTAIN THEIR INDIVIDUAL INTEGRITY AND STILL COPE TOGETHER TO FACILITATE AND PRESENT THE HIGHEST ETHICAL AND MORAL STANDARDS' OF SOCIOLOGICAL ORDER AND GOOD?"

POINT ONE: THE FATHER'S EXEMPLARY WISDOM, V.61:1

"There is no Wisdom, nor Understanding, nor Counsel against the Lord," Proverbs 21:30.

Sub-point: Predestined and "called" to salvation by the Holy Spirit, Ephesians 1:5.

The Kings and Priests of the Old Testament were anointed with oil for their Offices. Exodus 29:21, 40:13-15, Leviticus 8:12, 16:32, 2 Samuel 2:4, 5:3, 1 Kings 1:39.

"Whosoever shall be Great among you, let him be your Minister, and whosoever shall be Chief among you, let him be your servant," Matthew 20:26-27.

From the Old Covenant to the significant synecdoche components of the New Covenant, the demand for the Priestly educational pre-eminence of God likeness character with the anointing oil of the Holy Spirit for all leadership and commander mission statement vocations is an unchanging mandate, 1 Peter 4:17.

Illustrate: Genesis 3:15, inherited original sin and it's rudiments must resign themselves to the mortification's purgatorial dormitory for germicidal pre-emption of germination that begins at letter grade F, that by the transformative "law of faith's" cerebral process, growth and rising achieves and sustains the mastery of the incorruptible crown with letter grade A, 1 Corinthians 9:25, 1 Thessalonians 5:22.

Application: Focus on the student's "spiritual adoption equivalent" re-birth sanctification process, growth and rising steps protocol: For example, conception, gestation, fetal placenta nourishment, embryonic parishioner, parochial episcopal diocese, epitaph diadem epistle of "Romans 10:4 ceiling" ordination of papacy's encyclical panegyric, John 3:3-6, Hebrews 9:17, or the antithesis' spontaneous nature of the unregenerated fetus as self's mutilation from any nourishment, creating the proposed obstetrician's premature malpractice induced termination omission by spiritual hysterectomy, Hosea 9:11.

"The kingdom of God is like leaven, which a woman took and hid in three measures of meal, until the whole was leavened, simultaneously purging yourself of the old leaven of malice and hypocrisy, traversing the mortification of self's crucified flesh, by a transformative Spirit led vessel, manifesting a blamelessly irreproachable, empowered driven and nourishing oracle, fueled from the bread of life, operating as a perfected living epistle witness, speaking and reaching through the unleaven with sincerity and truth," Luke 13:20-21, 1 Corinthians 5:7-8, John 6:35-51, Colossians 3:5.

"For everyone who asks receives, and he who seeks finds, and to him who knocks it will be opened," Matthew 7:8.

"It is the Spirit who gives life; the flesh profits nothing. The words that I speak to you are spirit, and they are life," John 6:63.

"Wholly sanctify the tripartite; Body, Soul and Spirit," 1 Thessalonians 5:23, Hebrews 4:12.

"Man's terrestrial earthy natural body shall bear the image of the heavenly celestial body, raised in glory, power and incorruption by the resurrection and the life," 1 Corinthians 15:40, 44-47, John 11:25-26.

"For there are three that bear record in heaven: the Father, the Word, and the Holy Spirit, and these three are one. And there are three that bear witness on earth: the Spirit, the water, and the blood; and these three agree as one. If we receive the witness of men, the witness of God is greater; for this is the witness of God which He has testified of His Son," 1 John 5:7-9.

The identical theory and litany of the reasoning of knowledge, transcribing cognitive understanding formulations through the intellectual exercise with accountability mechanisms, that manifest promotional educational facets of freshman, sophomore, junior, too graduation senior obtaining your degree and Theological lawyer's bar-card, approved as a "Righteous man whose steps are ordered of the Lord, and whose seed is blessed evermore," Luke 13:19, Psalm 37:23-27.

"Let the riches of His glory, strengthen you with might through His Spirit in the inner man, being rooted and grounded in love and faith, that you may be able to comprehend with all the saints, what is the width and length and depth and height," Ephesians 3:16-18.

"The blind see, the maimed become whole, the lame walk, the lepers are cleansed, the deaf hear, the dead are raised, the poor have the gospel preached to them, and then the dumb speak, devils are cast out by prayer and fasting, the impoverished are empowered, employed and deployed to become apart of the global kingdom's governing body, that at the very least is fed, clothed and housed, and blessed is he who is not offended because of Me, as they glorify the God of Israel," Matthew 6:31-33; 15:31; 17:18-21, Mark 9:29, Luke 7:22-23.

"Letting no man despise thy youth, but being an example to the believers, in the Word, Conversation, Charity, Spirit, Faith, Purity," 1 Timothy 4:12.

"Speaking, thinking, understanding as a child, until Wisdom's maturity puts away childish things," 1 Corinthians 13:11.

"Trusted and heard the Word of Truth, after that, you believed and were sealed by the Holy Spirit of promise," Ephesians 1:13.

If you were physically born into the world, that is obvious material evidence of your predestination, and therefore, you are called to salvation by offering the voluntary will of your Tabernacle through presentation of the "Sheepfold" before the abiding "Door" of the blood atonement of the New Covenant's provision by verbally confessing your sins, and believing in your heart that God came in the flesh, lived a sinless life, was murdered and raised from the dead by the Father's Holy Spirit, for adherency's mortified obedience to that law and truth's dispensation of grace, that is primarily focused introspectively for promotion of a spiritual doctor lawyer expression toward generational perpetuity, that authoritatively deposes and dismantles the rule and pride of self's singular, unregenerated power, that restoratively and influentially procures transformation assimulated packaging for exaltation by the Holy Spirit's "washing of regeneration and the renewing of the mind" toward reciprocal justification, Leviticus 1:3, John 1:14, 6:53-54, Romans 10:8-13, Titus 3:5-7. Acts 4:12, 1 Corinthians 9:21.

"Lift up your heads to become an everlasting door," Psalm 24:7, John 10:1.

"You shall not curse the deaf, nor put a stumbling block before the blind, but shall fear your God; I am the Lord," Leviticus 19:14.

A blameless and harmless master teacher possesses the mercy of longsuffering toward process, growth and rising in a dispensation of grace, demonstrating a pattern of lasting good works with strategic teaching methodologies before a crooked and perverse nation of the ignorant and destitute, Luke 1:17, 1 Corinthians 9:19-22, Philippians 2:15, 1 Timothy 1:16, 2 Peter 3:16.

The middle partition now removed for the heirs of promise. The Old too signification of the New, (Ephesians 2:14-16), twain one new man of vicarious authoritative power and armorment of the personalized "Law of Faith's," contractual stipulations held instrumentally in trust and service, Romans 6:13, before the "law of an oath," Hebrews 6:17, to confirm the immutability of God's published Bible counsel/covenant and it's reciprocal trustworthiness as a strong consolation, Genesis 18:19.

"With the mind I myself serve the law of God, but with the flesh, the law of sin," Romans 7:25.

"If thou be wise, thou shall be wise for thyself, but if thou scornest, thou alone shall bear it," Proverbs 9:12.

It's 20 percent teacher instruction and influence, but 80 percent individualist hardwork of study and consecration. The rule normally being: Every 1 hour of classroom lecture, requires 5 hours of homework study, contemplation, meditation.

"Buy the truth, and sell it not, also wisdom, and instruction, and understanding," Proverbs 23:23, John 17:17.

"Blessed is the man who walks not in the counsel of the ungodly, Nor stands in the path of sinners, Nor sits in the seat of the scornful, But his delight is in the law of the Lord, And in His law he meditates day and night. He shall be like a tree planted by the rivers of water, that brings forth it's fruit in it's season, whose leaf also shall not wither, and whatsoever he does shall prosper," Psalm 1:1-3.

POINT TWO: THE SON'S EXEMPLARY DISCIPLINE, V.61:2

Sub-point: "Justified" by righteousness that thwarts the deaf, dumb and pervert demon, Matthew 11:5, 12:22.

"The serpent is more subtle than all the beasts of the field that God had made," Genesis 3:1. satanic confusion and ambiguity methods are camped on the antithesis line that's separating life from death, blessed from cursed, Deuteronomy 28:1-68. whose motive and intentions are cloaked in clever, aberrant notions and schemes that are premeditated influence design plays that are only detrimentally purposed to kill, steal and destroy, and are barely notice-able to the illiterate or blind eye rebel, without the illuminating mastery of judicious cutting edge holy precision understanding and impact, distinguishable from the masquerading "angel of light's," creeping infiltration of the seducing apocrypha doctrine of the demonic legion's only weapons; the distortions or elements that attempt to produce error against a sound conscience diagnosis of balanced judgment and influence, that has the potential of stumbling into heretical abstract disfigurement, like the "speaking lies in hypocrisy schism" leaven of the Pharisee's teaching presentation, cloaked as a righteous public minister, while simultaneously exacting a deviant subtle satanic inspiration permeating strategy of a private hypocrite's polluted judgment, discernment and equity against the destitute novice and their blind followers dying from poverty and retardation by the hands of a perceived leadership profligating of a practitioner's teaching impotence demands for slavery's letter, while simultaneously pimping for only threads and traces of it's own fudiciary responsibility of a balance of power and truth, manifesting internal mechanisms of a viral destitute motive and intent of a corpse like monster that is really purposed from the body of iniquity, and it's residual malignity of a seared conscience and it's nebulous distorted personality pervading the interpersonal relationship stratosphere manifesting from the lowest threshold as a "reverse evolutionist" headed toward a planet inhabited by apes, complicated by a buddhist's froward mouth and frivolous chicken scratches perfert exaltation of it's mentally ill rorschach test finding that illuminates a crown of ichabod, leperous sores on it's forehead, as a rabid dog manifestation, spiritually driven by a contagious dark cloudy atmospheric bacterial tuberculosis, not withstanding, in my view, the perfect investigation of the self-identified "God man," Proverbs 5:23, John 10:10, Acts 13:10; 17:22-23, 1 Corinthians 14:33, 2 Corinthians 11:14-15, 1 Timothy 4:1-2.

"That we should no longer be children, tossed to and fro and carried about with every wind of doctrine, by the trickery of men, in the cunning craftiness of deceitful plotting," Ephesians 4:14.

"Lest Satan get an advantage of us; for we are not ignorant of his devices," 2 Corinthians 2:11.

"Regard not them that have familar spirits, neither seek after wizards, to be defiled by them, I am the Lord your God," Leviticus 19:31; 20:27.

"And when they say to you, seek those who are mediums and wizards, who whisper, peep and mutter, should not a people seek their God? Should they seek the dead on behalf of the living?" Isaiah 8:19.

"The Righteousness of God is revealed from Faith to Faith. Thus, it is written, "the Just shall live by Faith." Romans 1:17.

The imulating duplicity of the already approved, tested and confirmed immutable infallibility of the authoritative Bible doctrine's covenant counsel is the plans and work of God, designed to be an abiding sustainable refuge, and "you cannot overthrow it, lest you even be found to fight against God," Acts 5:39, Romans 10:4.

Illustrate: The Ephesians 6:13-17 description of the full armor of God's, "helmet of salvation, breastplate of righteousness, belt of truth, shodding your feet with the preparation of the Gospel of Peace from the sword of the Spirit's power" put on and kept on, personifying the full stature as the perfect man, Ephesians 4:13.

The autopsy forensic results from the mortification of self's own flesh, with an exonerating, unindictable finding by all examining parties, deferring from either spiritual or material causes of action to proceed toward any jurisprudence judiciary that determines guilt and penalties, Romans 8:13.

Application: Spiritual warfare against subtle demonic radio-wave perversion temptations of the elements of the body of sin, which requires continuous mental posturing of the pre-eminent legal contract, New Covenant Counselor, not warring after the flesh, "casting down principalities, powers and dark imaginations and every high thought that tries to exalt itself against the knowledge of God's published will. Ephesians 6:12, 2 Corinthians 10:3-6.

Genesis 17:7 calls for reciprocal perfection from fusion with the Covenant that is called, "A God for thee," God is a Spirit, and adherents worship in Spirit-a symbol for the word that produces Truth, John 4:24. Therefore, the Head of the body is the Bible #3 Holy Spirit that in it's printed form remains a material quadraplegic until the freewill adherent begins the process, growth and rising steps protocol of transposing it's position, sequence and inactivity of #3 to the fullness of #2's vicarious representation's personification as the evidenced based presentation of the "end of the law for righteousness" theological justification as the first fruits of Monotheism, which is #1's delegated power, authority and Holy Spirit Word becoming spiritual adoption equivalent flesh and blood of the adherent, that you draw upon and perform judiciously with precision impact to purge the evil spiritual aberration from your thought patterns, to competently interface with all reality based equations, "storing up sound wisdom enabling the understanding of righteousness, judgment, and equity for every good path," Proverbs 2:9, without lifeless compromise of the major pre-requisites of ecclessiastical covenant and external lawfulness of commandments, absent perceptual reproach, even in the minors. Psalm 103:18, Romans 2:15, Galations 3:15, 1 Thessalonians 5:22.

"For in Him dwells all the fullness of the Godhead bodily; and you are complete in Him, who is the head of all principality and power," Romans 7:24, Colossians 2:9-10.

POINT THREE: THE HOLY SPIRIT'S EXEMPLARY MINISTRY, V.61:3

Historical evolutionary synecdoche of the Priesthood:

Historical understanding of the changed law of Old Testament Priesthood and Tabernacle protocol and service, now materially abolished, symbolizing the finished work of Christ by the intended perfection of a personalized Spiritual Tabernacle of the Soul and Spirit contained in a Body of Holiness for remission of sins and for a protectorate from wrath, to be "Blessed above all people," with eternal life, wisdom, health, prosperity and for conscience sake, Deuteronomy 7:12-15, Hebrews 9:6-7, by a God level High Priest and King example and by it's blood atonement, beyond the limitations of a methodology of gifts and sacrifices faulty unable to reconcile the mind from boasting in the singular element of simply keeping the law of circumcision; primarily designed as a sign of the initial Abrahamic Covenant with the following Mosaic Covenant concerning the creation of the knowledge of sin definitions, and their distinct differences, identifying Holy and unholy, clean and unclean concerning diverse washings, meats and drinks, carnal ordinances imposed until the time of reformation, empowering a degree of the superstitious indulging agnostic's own righteousness boasting, simply after the flesh, with a de-personalized willingness of self's ability to simply be proselytized by a pervasively compelled community acceptance from wrath provision, detached glory intermediary man formulation, rank structured by religious ceremony and animal blood officiating from the person's very own prepatory, direct access through the veil toward God into the "Holiest of all" as a personalized reciprocal container acquisition of a degree of the Glory's voice, cloud, and fire through their own individualist bodily temple; prophetically prognosticating for a vicarious imulation adherency exaltation through the veil of God's mortification standard of an emblematic crucified flesh, pardoned by the strength of Divinity's Blood atonement propitiation for a spiritually resurrected reciprocal personification that is empowered, anointed and commissioned for ambassadorship, Hebrews 7:12-16; 9:8-10, 1 Corinthians 6:20, 7:19, 2 Corinthians 4:7.

The historical Tabernacle and Temple timelines:

The Pentateuch authored: 1440 BC to Moses' death in approximately 1400 BC, with the remainder of the Old Testament completed by 440 BC.

The Tabernacle: From Mt. Sinai, about 1438 BC to 950 BC.

Solomon's Temple: 950 BC to 586 BC.

Zerubbabel's Temple: 444 BC to 20 BC.

Herod's Temple: 20 BC to AD 64.

27 books of the New Testament authored: AD 50 to AD 95; a 45 year period.

In summary: The 39 books of the Old Testament were authored over a 1000 year period, with an approximately 500 year gap between the completion of the Old and the fulfillment of the New, with it's transference of the Holy Spirit to the apostles for worldwide evangelism.

The harsh penalties, administered with a perceptually unbalanced commensuration by primordial antiquity's equity, with relationship to violations regarding the more ceremonial rules of the Pentateuch that was being delivered by the publicly known, Moses the "unadjudicated murdering man" from Mt.Sinai, who was subsequently anointing priests for service, may have in a few circumstances, invoked skepticism and murmuring in light of God's pronounced judgment in the wake of Genesis 6:13 "great violence through them," precedent of total destruction of the inhabitants of the earth, pertaining to vocational eligibility issues, and may have further inhibited the conscience by that chosen methodology and process as perceptually polluted and categorically discriminatory, that we obviously now know was prepatory evolution of historical events toward "the throne of grace," as a providentially assigned, (sinless) "once and for all blood atonement sacrifice," performed by God Himself in the flesh and blood image and likeness for the delegated power and provision to the freewill of a man's reciprocally embraced personification thereof, by a regenerated mind and circumcised heart believing unto righteousness, exercising a conscience void of offense toward God and man as a better surety toward a more fulfilling and excellent way, truth, and life's perfected covenant, primarily pertaining too the authenticity of the conscience, measured by a God pronounced "end of the law for righteousness standards package" for a sound mind, and a confident peace from deflected wrath, derived from being buried in baptism and then raised toward ascertaining a reciprocally embraced transformation empowering boldness from that prototype's provision and blessing for duplicated transference adherency, Genesis 1:26, Exodus 2:14; 4:19,24, 32:28,35, Acts 7:25, 24:16, Romans 2:29, Hebrews 4:14-16, Colossians 2:11-12.

For example, the seed of Aaron the Priest of that generation that had a "bodily blemish, blindness, lame, flat nose, or any thing superfluous, or a man that is brokenfooted, or brokenhanded, or crookbackt, or a dwarf, or that hath a blemish in his eye, or be scurvy, or scabbed or hath his stones broken" could not approach to offer offerings made by fire, or go in unto the vail, nor come nigh unto the altar as the Priestly service vocation, equating a potentially "sinless finding" with a material disease and or infirmity as being unworthy, profane and disqualifying to be an Old Testament, First Covenant Priest, Leviticus 21:17-23.

The necessity for a clarifying fulfillment prescription to enlist and emancipate for a massive Priestly Army, in addition too purging the conscience from the condemnation of dead works to serve the living God by the second Covenant's who-so-ever-will, John 3:16, pre-eminent qualifying spiritual manifesting personification of a God level example and resurrected body from the dead "champion person" in literal Holy Priesthood character form, beyond the inanimate, non-bodily transfiguration enigma of voice, cloud, fire or even the unprofitable weakness and designated shadow of carnal commandments contained in the law's flawed Levitical Priesthood system, after the order of Aaron, consisting of the delegated animal blood provision, Exodus 20:18, Micah 4:6-7, 2 Corinthians 12:9, Hebrews 7:18.

For example: cattle, a male without blemish, (herds: rams, bullocks), (flocks: goats and sheep), (fowls: turtledoves and pigeons), as burnt offerings, (peace offerings, whether male or female without blemish, breast: wave offering, right shoulder: heave offering), sin offerings, female lamb or kid of the goats, or two pigeons and two turtledoves, or a tenth part of an ephah of fine flour without any oil or frankincense, trespass offerings, and unleavened flour mingled with oil and frankincense called a meat offering seasoned with salt, and first fruits of grain offerings, green ears of corn dried by the fire, even corn beaten out of full ears. No leaven or honey was allowed for any burnt offering made by fire.

The offending person, or priest, elders for the congregration would by their voluntary will bring the offering and place their hand on the head of the animal sacrifice to be accepted as an atonement and kill it before the Lord at the door of the tabernacle of the congregration and the Priest that is anointed would then take of the blood, and bring it to the tabernacle of the congregation and the Priest would dip his finger in the blood, and sprinkle of the blood seven times before the Lord, before the vail of the sanctuary. And the Priest would put some of the blood upon the horns of the altar of sweet incense before the Lord, which is in the tabernacle of the congregation; and would pour all of the blood at the bottom of the altar of the burnt offering, which is at the door of the tabernacle of the congregation, although the sin offering has certain parts burnt and discarded "without the camp, where the ashes are poured out in a clean place" and the Priests would eat a fraction of some offerings, except the burnt offering which is wholly burnt, nor is the fat and blood eaten.

All of the offerings are pertaining too making atonement by the offending person's public confession for receiving forgiveness from sins through the anointed intermediary priestly vicarious ceremonial performance cleansing for sanctified consecration according to the instruction for each particular sin, Leviticus 1:1-7:38.

"For the Life of the flesh is in the blood, and I have given it to you upon the altar to make an atonement for your souls, for it's the Blood that makes atonement for the soul," Leviticus 17:11.

Also, mere men, like Moses the dictation stenographer man of the Pentateuch and angelic type messenger (Exodus 7:1), wasn't even allowed to see the "Face of Jehovah," beyond the transfiguration cloudy presence at the door of the tabernacle, unless he and or the people die," Exodus 33:20.

Or, by a religious ceremony of census taking, diverting wrath and plague from the congregation by offering half a shekel for atonement for their souls, Exodus 30:12-15.

Currency chart for Roman coinage and measurement:

One cubit equals: 17.5 inches.

One bekah equals: 1/2 shekel.

One shekel equals: 10-13 grams; 454 grams being 1 pound.

Twenty gerah equals: 1 shekel.

One mina equals: 50 shekels.

One talent equals: 3 thousand shekels or 86 pounds of silver or gold, equaling 6 thousand day's wages.

One denarius was a silver coin worth 18 cents, equaling 1 day's wages.

One mite was worth 1/8 of a cent.

Two mites equal a farthing.

One farthing or quadrant was worth 1/64 of a denarius.

One talent in U.S. currency would be about $108.00.

The detailed instructional discipline and culminating God intention was for: gathering and preparing a holy people and nation to be "The initial birthing epistle seed;" symbol for transformed living epistle from the house of Israel, beginning in the city of Jerusalem to ultimately be scattered to the entire earth in approximately AD 70, completing a prophetical journey of a non-blood line association from the Spirit, for the Father's promise to the immaculate conception of the clarifying lawgiver Jesus' blood atonement, primarily dealing with a pre-emptive, "pre-eminence theory" for the conscience, and for an ultimate spiritual transference toward who-so-ever-will transformation from evangelistic harvesting for spiritual adoption equivalency, as sustainable emulating duplication and multiplication of a perpetuated New Covenant influence directed toward all nations of the earth by "The commandment of the everlasting God, for obedience to the Faith," Genesis 28:13-14, Exodus 9:16, Psalm 50:2, Luke 24:47, Acts 1:8, 3:24-26, 10:28; 43-48, Romans 16:26, Colossians 1:18.

Jesus answered, "Most assuredly, I say to you, unless one is born of Water and the Spirit, he cannot enter the Kingdom of God," John 3:5.

"And the Word became flesh and dwelt among us, and we beheld His glory, the glory as of the only begotten of the Father, full of grace and truth," John 1:14.

The High Priest's entering into the Holy of Holies once a year, temporal ceremonial consecration purifying expiation of the sinful flesh for fulfilling the lusts therein, concerning the sinful ignorance of the Priest's and people, cleansed by the sprinkling of the blood of bulls and goats upon and before the mercy seat, in addition to the demand upon the people to keep carnal ordinances which stood only in circumcision, intended only as an initial sign of a prepatory covenant, including meats and drinks, divers washings imposed upon them by the first Covenant until the time of reformation, validating the prepatory nature of the insufficiency of the continuous revolving door of animal blood that really couldn't convince the conscience that a propitiation was solidified, or even the inanimacy, delivered by "the disposition of angels," the instructions obtained and delivered through obviously the flawed man Moses, who subsequently died wandering around in the wilderness for 80 years as a covert fugitive from justice, until he reached the age of 120 years old, the age limit that was imputed upon mankind right before the great flood, God's reasoning was because of great violence upon the earth, "through them," Genesis 6:13, and for the sons of God involved in the intermarriage with the daughters of men, "unequally yoked," Genesis 6:2-7. 2 Corinthians 6:14.

The record indicates in Exodus 2:11 that Moses, by his own hand was guilty of unlawfully killing an Egyptian, and was under a death penalty indictment by the present Pharaoh.

Furthermore, the 40 year wilderness penalty designation imputed by God Himself, intended as a rejection and death penalty against all of the adult Israelites, twenty years or older, judged as murmuring transient fugitives, whose dead carcasses would never enter the promised land, (only the remaining seed of the dead, and Caleb and Joshua would enter the land of Canaan), that was presently occupied and had become a stronghold, inhabited by the Amalekites and Canaanites, Numbers 14:22-34, Deuteronomy 32:51.

God's lofty standards, confirmed through His infinite nature and integrity methods of the Oath, Law, and Covenant to communicate and confirm the immutability of His counsel toward creation, in regards to His irrespectability of persons, providentially chosen or otherwise, places a "no tolerance for error policy" upon the established leadership Priesthood, providing a healthy incentive and pressure to produce competence, mastery and God likeness perfection or suffer the humiliating consequences and defeat of becoming another historical statistic, sanctimonious encroachment diagnosis as "God's ensamples" of published dishonor grandstanding of evidentiary substantive commensuration penalizing degrees and or death's sting for defilment, evidenced and transcended by literary precedent, with the prophetic synecdoche from Old to New.

Thus, in my view exonerating from a negative God ensample's identity crisis of heretical aberrations cloaked and sequestered behind sarcophagus sepulchers prognosticating and even legitimizing a "perfect marathon investigation" by the Pharisee's hypothesizing their aboriginal status' first Covenant God authority before the midst of large crowds amassing, drawn by intermittent transient miracles challenging their fearless, responsible fiduciary nature, without abeyance or abdication by risking their own death for an investigative miscalculation, defending against possible idolatry deviating; (the Jews sought to kill him for violating the sabbath and a polytheistic power grab) that seems to have produced problematic evidence by their sustained life in the midst of touching the very person of God, beyond the enigma of voice, cloud and fire measured by historical precedent at Mt. Sinai for indictable analogy hypocrisy leaven in this particular case that was permeated with hearsay and perceptual God contradiction by the ambiguous mystery blinding of "history writing in the making;" further measured by their inability from inferential dialogue understanding acknowledgment as finite men to close shop on animal sacrifices that were originally ordered by God Himself, (Mark 12:32-34), and that only a real God could correct any symbolizing shadowy type weakness and unprofitable synecdoche that really couldn't perfect anyone's conscience as a rite of reciprocal consolating beyond the detached external rituals and dietary laws pertaining to inner holiness and cleanliness issues identifying and contrasting clean and unclean spirits relationally pointing to the depth and understanding of their true intent and applications effecting mental stability, health related issues and influentially solidifying its pre-eminent material legal standing from the strength of its spiritually pardoned authority, evolving toward the Kingdom of God's geocentric fulfillment of a personally demonstrated sinless God standard's package, concluded by an emblematic blood atonement sprinkling for a consciousness from wrath reconciliation provision by self examination auditing for reciprocal transformation emulating personalized authenticity of a tripartite God likeness priestly lordship through who-so-ever-will's Body, Soul, and Spirit, culminating the two primary divisions of predestination from the heavenly record of Father, Word and Holy Spirit for a perpetuity witness as Spirit led, by the Water of the Word and it's Blood atonement personification as "the end of the law for righteousness to those who believe it," (Leviticus 20:27; 26, John 10:33) Matthew 22:36-40; 23:2-3, Mark 8:31-38; 13:10,22; 15:32,36,38, Luke 5:21-24, John 1:13; 2:18-21; 3:9, 14-15; 5:18; 8:58; 9:29; 11:49-52, Acts 10:34-35; 17:26, Romans 10:4, 1 Corinthians 10:11, Colossians 3:25, 1 Thessalonians 5:23, Hebrews 4:12, Titus 1:15-16, 1 John 5:7-9.

"And also of the Son of the Bondwoman will I make a nation, because he is thy seed," Genesis 21:13.

"And thou shall say unto Pharaoh, thus says the Lord, Israel is My Son, even My first born," Exodus 4:22, Psalm 2:7-8.

"Therefore, by the deeds of the (first Covenant's Priestly Law of circumcision, animal sacrifices, diverse washings) shall no flesh be justified, for by the law is the knowledge of sin. But now the righteousness of God is revealed without that law, witnessed by the Law and the Prophets," Romans 3:20-21.

Primarily setting up the law as a restraint mechanism for free-will agents by the first Covenant, subsequent to creation, pertaining to the soul and the flesh, with a prophetical future mandate to include the enhanced ability to thwart penalties creating mental anguish scars, and even beyond just the singular immediacy of a flawed deliverance provision from a psyche bondage by transgression from the Old Testament to maintaining the potential for deliverance from the law's material wrath through the same standard against sin in a more fulfilling New Testament, which would eventually be animatedly attained, personalized, solidified by the second Covenant's pre-emptive spiritual calibration and acquisition of the promise of Faith by consecrated sanctification of the holiness and righteousness of the "law of liberty and the spirit of life's" culminating ceiling of righteousness standards' package of reality for perfection, would bring eternal pardon to enable and bring a boldness and confidence to the spirit-man from serving the end of the law for righteousness, that would bring freedom to the repenting fugitive and vagabond and bring closure to the conscience of the soul from the bondage of indignation, wrath, anguish, tribulation, putrid sores, wounds, bruises, and defend even the material body from the potential wrath of disease, Exodus 15:26, 23:25, Deuteronomy 28:21,22, and or the investigative revenger, Psalm 8:2, Romans 13:2, by it's blamelessly irreproachable unified posture of a tripartite form of spirit, water and blood, exonerating from both the spiritual and material manifestations of the law of sin and the fear of punishment or death; "For to live is Christ, and to die is gain," 2 Chronicles 7:14-22, Luke 1:74-75, Philippians 1:21, 1 Timothy 1:9-10, Hebrews 2:15, 1 John 5:8.

The Bondmaid and the Freewoman are an allegory of the two Covenants, Galatians 4:23-24.

Becoming grafted into a kingdom as a spiritual living epistle Church's bodily member in a personalized, transposed God level ministerial example word becoming spiritual adoption and demonstrated functionality of the emulating equivalent of the new royal Priestly state's ceiling of reality as the end of the law for righteousness for those who believe it, with wisdom's synthesizing recognition of theological pre-eminence in all mission statement's material Constitutionality, with the silent veil between Church and State only relevant to aberrations from the proper interpretation of the "Law of Faith," without extracting the "pre-eminence theory" of ecclesiastical administration of character and it's depth of ethical and moral policy operation of Influence, even in Government, 2 Corinthians 3:15.

"Every purpose is established by counsel, and with good advice make war," Proverbs 20:18.

The separation of Church and State really means: "You wouldn't want to regulate away from the irrefutable objective realities of the theological preeminence formulating standards' of competence, mastery and perfection's ethical and moral precision, relative to the spiritual individual character effecting the material organizational mission statement's business reciprocity toward profit and success," Proverbs 8:15-16, Isaiah 44:9, Acts 12:23, 1 Corinthians 12:7-11.

"Render therefore to Caesar the things that are Caesar's, and to God the things that are God's, exacting no less than appointed," Matthew 22:21, Luke 3:13.

"Do not hurt the Oil and the Wine," Revelation 6:6.

Symbols of the theologically approved and permissive activities of the two primary instruments or swords of Christianity's Holy Spirit empowered administrative operations, separated by distinct and contrasting mission statement vocations; although, designed for the same motive, intent, and purpose, relating to either the Priestly Office's Spiritual (war, "oil") officiating to pre-empt evil by self examination auditing, with also a spiritually significant sociological link to the Kingly Office's material investigative "policing minister revenger," Military (war, "wine") officiating, with both defending against spiritual failure, without obstruction, by thwarting or diminishing an elevated material transgressing threat toward life and or property, Romans 13:4, 1 Corinthians 12:5-6, 2 Chronicles 6:34-35.

Theological justifications: Historical theory of God's man of war for the 21st century Minister Revenger:

"Where there is no law, there is no violation of law," Romans 4:15.

Israel's 603,550 "men of war" separated by (ensign: A ranked commissioned military officer's standard): Meaning mission statement vocation of material war, translated into 21st century applicable interpretation from the rooted depth of the Bible's spiritual and material prerequisite admonishments to hate evil and destroy the body of sin, executing the complexity formulations and methodology of intellectual preliminary criminal Investigative scope, realm and domain, including standard rhetorical soliloquy statement's "verbalized hypothesized reverse osmosis mirror counteracting against a stealth infringement's demonic depravity," with A-level acting policing investigative dragnet fishing reel containing visceral vernacular ventriloquist's voice inflected rememberance promptings and or reading of a police report containing a criminal's epithets, or the dictionary defined word: bitch; Meaning a female dog or complaining, or Bible words such as bastard; Meaning fatherless and transient, or ass; Meaning donkey, or (shit-tim; Meaning a type of wood for building, Exodus 26:15) being rhetorically pronounced and exercised by an undercover police officer actor as a survivalist's methodology of a bait, mark and netting authority for manufacturing evidentiary substance with a use of force policy's permissive bellicose indignation type rhetoric, germane against a perfidious adversary already identified as the purported poltergeist exorcist's obstreperous excrement lacking any authority or legal standing, of which criminal sin of a monster's "hide, flesh and dung is burned outside the camp," Leviticus 8:17, Numbers 2:2; Hebrews 13:11, which would mean:

"Unclean irreverent satanic power in opposition too, and petitioning for the incapacitation of the God ordained delegated power of the Administration of Justice system," Mark 3:30, 32-35.

"The evil spirits even recognize Jesus as the record from heaven, and Paul as the witness upon the earth," Acts 13:6-11; 19:15.

For example, the same theory and depth of the theological preeminence in the 21st century mission statement vocation representation of the Administration of Justice system as God's Minister revenger of internally hating evil and destroying the personified body of criminal level sin through complexity formulating methodogies as a hostage negotiator and it's SWAT team member under the auspices of California law, and the theological protectorate of Exodus 21:13, waiting for a lawful "lethal-force green light order" doesn't really have any intention to allow the criminal to escape from justice, and may even mask a lie, assigned as rhetorical soliloquy statements in order to bait and mark for apprehension and or save life or property from damage.

Thus, the symmetrical superlative rhetoric is a justifiable warfare methodology without obtrusively staining your own conscience or blemishing a sanctified vessel within that mission statement's colored authority and delegated customary rules, including a "use of Force policy, beginning with verbal rhetoric, that commensurately authorizes, one step above the adversary, up to deadly force," justifying the motive, intent, purpose and mission of the agent against declared war, activating the mandatory vicarious statutory authorization to thwart the adversary's spiritual failure, cloaked as a statutory violation, manifesting sophisticated, presumptuous diabolical malice, aforethought and guile as a material transgressing threat toward potentially persons or property, specifically pertaining to the complexity formulations synthesizing impossibility of divorcing the multiple elements designed equation of 1) a statutory motive and intent, 2) linked to the exigency of probable cause, 3) with the theological and legal justifications of the ensign's standard psychological assimulations and "free-lancing" cloaked in rhetorical soliloquy, verbalized hypothesizing reverse osmosis mirror to bait, mark and net for a criminal arrest, 4) especially when the criminal presentation locks itself into an agent's overtly objective scientific empirical data of the peace officer power, probable cause, use of force policy zone, deducing the impossibility of any civil liability or any cause of action, as explicitly stated in the law against an Officer's reasonable suspicion delegated to a statutory job duty, measured against cloaks and veiled evidence of a criminal's alleged celebrity big name and title being invalidated by a lack of authority or legal standing detection in statutory identified transgression realm and domain to mitigate from their infringement liabilities pertaining to "high crimes or misdemeanors" or to empower any sort of aberrant illegal perversion of the already established Administration of Justice system and protocol of the complexity formulas and equations that are already legislatively implicit and explicitly rhetorical as set and contained in the proper context of the policeman's colored authority engagement to snapshots and moments, that could never psychologically inhibit or diminish the officer's mandatory vicarious lawful authority counteracting methodologies against any name, title, entity, thereby substantiating the theological and legal pre-eminence of liability shielding and officer safety issues, especially in the preliminary stage of investigation.

A lawless government entity and it's unscrupulous rogue stealth representation on an aberrant fishing expedition attempting to create a statutory violation, with a phony warrant or without a warrant that is detected in statutory identified transgression realm and domain that is crashing into any other law enforcement agency's lawful complexity formulations cloaked in rhetorical soliloquy, verbalized hypothesizing voice inflected ventriloquism promptings from the authority of a statutory motive and intent to bait, mark and net policing authority counteracting against a terrorist equivalent could only be measured as a degree and facet of the Holy Spirit's competence, mastery and perfection's justification personified as God's Minister investigative revenger for a reverse osmosis mirror of relevant discovery information, petitioner's warrant for their interagency governmental impeachment, arrest, and prosecution.

The elementary school law enforcement theory, principles and concepts to confirm competence, mastery and perfection's justification wouldn't necessarily mitigate the criminal's unknown motivating adversarially perceived psychotic behaviors that are well over the line and out of bounds of the normal security protocol relating to the normal course of business operations, and specifically linked and pertaining to the Santa Clara County Department of Correction law enforcement agency component of the peace officer powers being exercised and empowered by a custodial officer's three layers of probable cause against: 1) breach of the institution's 5 layer security protocol, 2) grand theft of intellectual properties transposed by the stealth infringement suspects from it's intended effect as law enforcement activity into the global economy for a DOW ten thousand entertainment, 3) prepping for, or attempted murder against a custodial officer under the color of police authority, that couldn't possibly be deemed an acceptable or trustworthy platform for any type of legitimate negotiations other than the investigative, policing activity against the "suicide by cop" criminal presentation, Luke 14:31;

Contrasted from the Levitical Priests focus on individual pre-emptive self examination auditing, cloaked as the clergy's spiritual war officiating, Numbers 1:46-54, Deuteronomy 20:12.

"There are, it may be, so many kinds of voices in the world, and none of them is without significance. Therefore, if I do not know the meaning of the voice, I shall be a barbarian to him who speaks, and he who speaks will be a barbarian to me," 1 Corinthians 14:10-11.

"Therefore let him who speaks in a tongue pray that he may interpret. For if I pray in a tongue, my spirit prays, but my understanding is unfruitful. What is the conclusion then? I will pray with the spirit, and I will pray with the understanding. I will sing with the spirit, and I will also sing with the understanding."

Juxtaposition the parallel of self's expression and relationship to it's corporate body's discipline for spiritual edification with the "just balances and measurements" mandate of a comprehensively sustaining self examination auditing, beginning with psychological construction from authoritative sources for context centered verbal rhetoric justification of blameless interpretation and application from the focused theory and depth derivatives derived from the theological prerequisite's apprehension of the living epistle formulations and adherency consummation of the linguist's understanding, judgment and discernment as the starting point for competence, mastery and perfected vocational policing mechanism's synthesizing equation of a bait, mark and netting authority for the manufacturing and packaging of lawfully sustainable evidentiary substance, without remorse or reproach, 1 Corinthians 14:13-15.

"All the ways of a man are clean in his own eyes, but the Lord weigheth the spirits by just balances and measurements," Proverbs 16:2,11.

"The Spirits of the Prophets are subject to the Prophets," 1 Corinthians 14:32.

"A divine sentence is in the lips of the King, and He transgresseth not in judgment," Proverbs 16:10.

For example: The pre-eminent didactic doxology catechism drama dragnet of the state's version, recognized by the Bible as: the superscription and image of ordination certificate of California Penal Code section 831.5 (f) (g)1; revised in September 1999 to include warrantless misdemeanor and felony investigative jurisdictional policing authority and arrest powers being exercised by a custodial officer with specific entity targeting of inmates, visitors and relevant persons within it's scope, realm and domain of enforcing ordinances and statutes relating to breaches of the institutional security's protocol and infrastructure, such as attempted lynching and or terrorist attacks, with pertinent penal code sections applicable to extraneous defense postured policing during the operations of transportation and guarding hospitalized inmates, including investigation of principles and accessories involving escape pursuits, with all other integral community policing conducted while maintaining custody and order of the correctional facility's incarcerated population contained within a county's jurisdictional providence of a city. Penal code section 830.1(c) also defines a correctional officer as an "on duty only" California peace officer. Also 830.55(a-e) stipulated by the presence of parole violators being detained and or county or city facilities that maintain custody of inmates defined under certain sections would legally apply to the public officer being a peace officer designation in those circumstances. The limited required training is the same for the public or limited duty peace officer designations under the aforementioned penal code sections constraining the limitation and scope of duties to the correctional officer job classification mandate of the 832 pc training and the 6035 Board of Corrections standard provisions, without the full POST academy. In other words, you can still deputize a public officer a limited duty exercising peace officer in the state of California and still retain the pay disparity between full duty peace officers and limited duty peace officers which is really the budgetary motive of the hiring agency and the intent of the legislation.

"Caesar's taxes" for the character of God's investigative revenger, that linguistically translates from Church and State perspectives as:"

"Resisting the ordained powers and ordinance of God brings damnation," or a policing type taxation, Romans 13:2, Matthew 22:19-21.

"Therefore submit yourself to every ordinance of man for the Lord's sake, whether to the King as supreme, or to Governors, as to those who are sent by him for the punishment of evildoers and for the praise of those who do good. For this is the will of God, that by doing good you may put to silence the ignorance of foolish men," 1 Peter 2:13-15.

"Especially those who walk according to the flesh in the lust of uncleanness and despise government; they are presumptuous, self-willed. They are not afraid to speak evil of dignities," 2 Peter 2:10.

"If any being is marked by sin, he himself shall drink of the wine of the wrath of God, which is poured out full strength into the cup of His indignation. He shall be tormented with fire and brimstone," Job 10:14, Lamentations 3:42, Revelation 14:9-10.

Therefore, the unambiguous link is certified between the apocalyptic power source delegating rules to a "being's character performance" of material reality's Administration of Justice system for pre-emptive individual literacy mastery of lawfulness, self-control and the excellency of competence as a degree and facet of the Holy Spirit, absent from lawless presumption or lying in wait, malice, aforethought, guile, that is consecrated by allowing the mysterious theological theory of spiritual police officer Bible to reciprocally measure a person by self-examination auditing for holiness acquisition and integrity's preservation, with apprehension, and extraction of the character flaws of evil pervert, mentally ill, and incompetent dissimulation from it's mission statement's colored authority mandate of authoritative equations and their complexity formulating methodologies reaching through the fog of a war zone with the theory and depth of theological justification and legality toward profit and success, 2 Timothy 2:21.

"The fear of the Lord is to hate evil, pride, arrogancy, the evil way and a forward mouth," Proverbs 8:13.

"And that ye may put difference between Holy and unholy, clean and unclean," Leviticus 10:10.

VS. the public reproach, humiliation of the chronic bacterial spiritual disease analogy from a material leprosy diagnosis of "having a running issue from the flesh that is pronouced unclean," Leviticus 15:2.

"The leprosy plague is in his head," Leviticus 13:44.

"The Lord shall smite thee with madness, blindness and astonishment of heart," Deuteronomy 28:28, equated and diagnosed from being slothfully unlearned, slothfully undisciplined, and slothfully unindustrious.

The applicability has relevance toward damnation, market value depreciation, financial loss from the unqualified state of the destitute or potential transgressor, being materially policed by supernatural powers and or it's instruments of Penal Code, Business and Professions Code, Civil Code, indictment, lawsuit, etc. creating a perpetual negative influence problem and burden upon the economy of prestige, "to the third and even fourth generation," Exodus 20:5, Deuteronomy 5:9, Psalm 109:13-15, Hebrews 11:4).

Wisdom's precocious precision journey is suppose to be toward perfection: "God's people are precariously predisposed to perish for lack of the Priestly preeminent knowledge," Hosea 4:6.

Sub-point: "Chosen" for holiness, 1 Timothy 3:1-7.

Illustrate: The standards of the New Covenant bishop is ordained as the universal standards as the "end of the law for righteousness" to those who believe it's spiritual pre-eminent authority that internally hates evil and either spiritually and or materially destroys the personified body of sin through diversity and methodology of operations and administrations, derived from the interpretive totality of understanding the New Covenant's rooted depth and stream that is manifestly postured, thwarting the prodigal that is competently commissioned for leadership command as Christ's prodigy of prodigious character procuring performance based meritorious commendations that are continually entreating for maturity's self examination auditing and peer review receptivity for personal and organizational censure, correcting and challenging for the New Covenant's ascertainable perfection of the apprenticeship's faith of the potentate for the promises, Luke 6:40, Romans 10:4, Acts 17:31, Revelation 2:1-29; 3:1-22; that the least member, as part of the body should strive for, eleviating the totality of the whole body from perceptual blots through the corporate vicarious sinful influence of being slothfully unlearned, slothfully un-disciplined, and slothfully un-industrious, 1 Corinthians 12:26.

"Judgment pre-eminently begins in the house of the Lord, and through the vessel of the Lord," 1 Corinthians 2:15, 1 Peter 4:15-17.

"The new wine must be put into new wineskins, and both are preserved" by the synecdoche's reciprocal adherency for the promises, Psalm 119:80-83;96, Mark 2:22.

"The righteous shall never be removed, but the wicked shall not inhabit the Earth," Proverbs 10:30.

"Not slothful in business, fervent in Spirit, serving the Lord," Romans 12:11.

Contrast the "bondage, rejection and curse of the weak and beggarly elements" of thorns, thistles, briers, tares, whose end is to be burned; manifesting and choking for the pre-eminence as a delusional competitive counterfeiting rooted gall of pernicious bitter failure as the forbidden poisonous fruit of the body of sin, Deuteronomy 29:18, Matthew 13:36-40, Luke 8:14, Galations 4:9, Hebrews 6:8.

"Destroy the body of sin," Romans 6:6,

The three primary classifications that sin is derived from: Ecclesiastical, civil and criminal, with each category containing a division of levels, degrees and sub-divisions requiring variations of evidence and proof. Opposing yourself through failure, ignorance or the willful and premeditated craftiness, equivalent to a dark cloud of malice and aforethought toward commission of violating the provisions thereof carries an effectual judgment for spiritual and material commensuration type sanctions or wrath penalties, of which severity is defined by each specific governing code, Deuteronomy 25:1, Matthew 5:23-26, Acts 18:14-17, Romans 2:12, 2 Timothy 2:25-26, 1 John 5:17.

"Murders, thefts, perjury, strife, inventor's of evil things, backbiters, revilers, filthy communication, wickedness, maliciousness, malignity, whispering gossipers, disobedience to parents, implacable, covenant breaker's, without natural affection, unmerciful, hater's of God, deceitful, without understanding Proverbs 9:10, (the holy synthesize knowledge into understanding), doubtful disputations, vanities, debates, avoiding foolish questions, genealogies, contentions and strivings about the law that are unprofitable and vain, Titus 3:9, through casting pearls before swine and dogs that don't really want to learn anything, but simply want to strangle the messenger, or misinterpretation, incompetence, corruption, slander, receiving an accusation against an elder without two or three legitimate witnesses, traitors, brutish pastors Jeremiah 10:21, preaching any other gospel, failure to evangelize the world by rightly dividing the word of truth, causing others to stumble in their faith through words, actions or wrong lifestyle influence, revelers, denying material and spiritual support and leadership to your own wife and children; (holy, mature masterful leadership has the skill and longsuffering fortitude to preserve the family unit intact, without forsaking its sanctity, 1 Timothy 5:8), in addition and including assistance out of your abundance of the same, if it is within your power, toward spiritually defined family members of mother or brother grafted into the "Body of Christ," loveless, anger, no striker, not self-willed, sedition, tumults, swellings, malice, pride, arrogance, wrath, hatred, envy, jealousy, coveting, extortion for filthy lucre, bribery against the innocent, oppressing an employee from fair wages, injustice, idolatry (angels are not worthy of worship), heresy, sorcery, witchcraft, cowardice, (the doctrine of Balaam and the Nicolaitans: whoremongering, licentious, lewd, or premeditated participation of eating meats offered up among idolaters enjoining idols, in addition to eating blood, things strangled; beasts that die of themselves, Acts 15:20, 1 Corinthians 6:9-10; 8:7, Revelation 2:14-15, homosexuality; the shittim wood that the Old Testament Tabernacle was built with is an allegorical indictment against the suckers and sodomites, effeminate, fornication, adultery), drunkeness, lazy and gluttonous toward obesity and poverty, variance into dissimulation from appropriate emulation, (justification begins in the Holy Spirit and manifests the Holy Spirit and sustains the Holy Spirit), hating brethren without a cause is discord type murder already, lusting in the mind is adultery in the heart already, fallen demon spirits are judged already, hidden iniquity is spiritual failure, separation and alienation from God in the secret place's of the mind and heart that can produce the viral infection of the bad fruit of civil and or criminal trespassing as well, omission of emergency necessity toward neighbor, abusing and or neglecting the widow, fatherless, and destitute victim, stranger, and or repentant, opposing themselves, forsaking the assembly of fellowship with other networking believers as a continual strengthening and accountability mechanism, abusing themselves with mankind, any other thing that is contrary to sound doctrine, including the six things the Lord specifically hates, yes even seven are an abomination to him: 1) A proud look, Pharisee image, rebels against appropriate authorities, and or a failing novice image, 2) A lying tongue, 3) A heart that devises wicked imaginations, 4) Hands that shed innocent blood, 5) Feet that are swift in running to evil, 6) A false witness who speaks lies, 7) One who sows discord among the brethren," Deuteronomy 21:20, Proverbs 23:21, Romans 1:29-32, Galatians 5:19-21, 2 Timothy 3:2-5, Proverbs 6:16-19.

The premeditated entertaining and postured mentality of plotting evil; "these things come from within and defile a man;" not merely a disregard for external rituals and dietary laws, Mark 7:15-23.

"These are waterless clouds tossed about by every wind, brute beasts and barbarians feeding themselves without fear, a fruitless tree, without fruit, twice dead and plucked up from the root, raging waves of the sea foaming out their own shame, wandering stars reserved in the blackness of judgment forever. These are spots in your feasts of charity, Jude 1:25, wrinkles, blemishes, tarnishes that banish the dog returning to it's vomit, or the sow that was washed returning to the mire." The whitewashed tomb of a Pharisee's corruption, aberrant motives and intents, purpose and mission that is satanically inspired. The chained leper weeping in the ashes of torment and the outer darkness of a sewer, that gnashes their teeth in blind, rebellious indignation as they gaze upon themselves in the dim mirror of an image and likeness of a "monster's dung" smeared like plaster on self's very own manufactured wedding garment that has a marriage certification appointment with spiritual death, reserved for the alien's detached domain, despair and destruction, Malachi 2:3.

Recognizing only one antithesis line formulated by multiple antonym's of contrasting description of the "Body of Holiness" and the body of sin," we draw upon Psalm 103:18 pertaining to keeping the covenant and commandments, and Leviticus 26 penalties for the clarity of supernatural and interpersonal indictments against personified idolatry in representation and or the presentation of the "body of sin."

"And the Lord said unto Moses, whosoever hath sinned against Me, him shall I blot out of My book," Exodus 32:33, Revelation 3:5.

"I will punish you seven times for your sins and send seven times the plague upon you, your highways shall be desolate, your threshing shall not reach it's vintage and your vintage shall not reach it's sowing time, your strength shall be spent in vain, (continuous spiritual and material famine), the Heaven shall not bring forth it's rain, (spiritual and material drought), your Heaven shall be like iron and your Earth brass, wild beasts shall come into the land and you shall eat the flesh of your son's and daughter's, or (the cannibalism of generational curses relating to a bad name in reputation), ten women shall bake your bread and divide it's portions by weight and you shall not be satisfied, the land nor the fruit tree shall yield it's fruit and you shall not eat of the new because of the old, (the seed contained in the fruit for continuous cycles of harvesting), your heart shall become faint and you will flee when no one is pursuing you, as the perception of a shaking leaf chasing one fleeing from a sword and you shall not be able to stand in the presence of your enemies in the day of adversity and shall fall by their sword, reprobate paranoid indignation, wrath, anguish, tribulation within the seared consciousness of the guilty mind and heart, a strong delusion, the power of five chasing one hundred and one hundred putting ten thousand of your enemies to flight shall not prevail, I will bring the power of the sword against you and avenge the quarrel of my covenant, literal material war in every context, terror, consumption, (burning ague: fever with recurrent chills and sweating or malaria) shall consume the eyes and cause sorrow of heart. They that hate you, shall rule over you. Your cities shall be waste and your sanctuary desolate."

We understand the aforementioned causes directly relate to the divine inference of nature's superiority to be one effectual extraneous response or effect against the unreformed "body of sin" walking contrary to the Covenant of God, but also the effect of peer review responses, (Investigative revenger) against the metaphorical depth of bacteria as a perceptual spiritual reproach, leper defined type penalties of quarantine and social death, relating to the disposition and demeanor of self-destructive internal spiritual mechanisms that qualify by unrestrained material deadness of pre-existing root systems warring against God's influential covenant of preemptively designed, introspective calibrating of measured synthesized contextual wisdom of the intellect and senses; temperance, courage, judgment, justice and equity, exalted by the individualist responsibility of achieving the ceiling of holiness and righteousness parameter's, by self examination, acquisition and an exercising, sanctifying preservation that skillfully evolves from the infant's initial ability to handle and grasp the understanding of a babe's "milk" toward apprehension of maturity's, fullness, wholeness and completeness of the judicial pardoning strength that receives, comprehends and embraces the deepest and highest quality of reality from the "meat of the Word," John 6:27; Hebrews 5:13-14.

In most cases, the reprobate criminal mind is focused willfully and intently within their consciousness of guilt on their own poisonous fruit by either elementally defined spiritual ecclesiastical sins unto death and or the statutory violations fused in their mind with the presence of their crime scene, with a singleness of thoughtfully prioritized exigency of self preservation, disposal and diversion methods stealthy postured in a dark cloud of malice and aforethought, especially when their pretense, livelihood and or freedom is threatened by direct examination and the radar scrutiny of authoritative sources.

In contrast, the holy mind is open and transparent and focused intently on the pre-emptive elementally fruitful literacy of the lawful New Covenant, the capsulation as the extended olive branch derived from the types, symbols, shadows and prophetical depth, trans-mortifying a purified offering as the preferred succession from prefaced significance of the Old Covenant's prepatory procuring of the timeless preserving salty ingredient's (Leviticus 2:13) that "eternalizes" the agent of God's Holy personified voluntary-will assimilation and predictive preeminence manifesting the infallible hypothesis of the theorized spiritual evolution of sanctification through a continuous measuring judgment of intellectual exercising of selfless glorified mental posturing status that willfully, intentionally and masterfully, by process, growth and rising, methodically forges ahead and disposes of self's own lawless motives, intents, purpose and mission of carnality that is God defined opposition headed toward insanity and destruction, while postulating a reconstructed image and likeness of a blamelessly irreproachable living epistle formulation that can then make appropriate interpersonal reciprocity investments, business computations, evaluations, and stand confidently before any enemy in it's unindictable, spiritually solidified material form, realm, domain and existence that authoritatively and conclusively exemplifies and profligates an influence and perfection throughout the landscape and economy of the world; "Bearing a vessel in sanctification and honor," 1 Thessalonians 4:4.

Impleading with the soldiering, farming and shepherding of all of the elements and fruit of Christ's Body of Holiness and Righteousness, making your calling and election by grace a better surety, 1 Corinthians 9:7, 2 Timothy 2:3,6,10, 2 Peter 1:4,10,11: The Kingdom's expression manifested bodily through the priestly member's office, and delegated sociologically linked political government administrations and operations, including the defense postured Military, policing war office entities that are either officiating their own mission statement vocational discipline, derived from an executive, legislative and judicious checks and balances protectorate of maintaining the "appointed safety zone" of the theological prerequisites of a God righteousness character administration that is constant and blameless, even during "actual material war time events," absent from lawless lying in wait, guile, malice, aforethought; being un-associated with the treachery of a lack of lawful authority that administers a disposition of injustice, while simultaneously being spiritually sustained and strengthened by it's pre-eminently postured worship ministry relating to competence, mastery and perfection through lifestyle and vocation, in concert with fellowship, discipleship, evangelism, that is facilitated and administered primarily through the corporate and mobile Church of individual vessels by a diversity of gifted methodologies through it's elected officer's described as; apostles, prophets, pastors, evangelists, teachers, elders, and the perfected saints infused, rooted and solidified with one Lord's mind, will and Holy Spirit's Oath, Law and Covenant, Exodus 21:13-14, Jeremiah 3:15, Ephesians 4:10-12, Acts 2:38.

"Pure and undefiled religion before God and the Father is this; to visit orphans and widows in their trouble, and to keep oneself unspotted from the world," James 1:27.

"He sent Redemption unto His people, He has Commanded His Covenant forever: Holy and Reverend is His name," Psalm 111:9.

For those who don't participate in the eucharist communion, or eat the symbols of body and drink the Blood of the Lord unworthily, risk eternal life and bring damnation upon themselves, as "many are weak, sick and dead among you, because of yielding to sin, satan and self's reciprocal stronghold presentation as the deaf, dumb, and pervert demon," 1 Corinthians 11:27-29, John 6:54. Romans 5:9.

A) The Ten Commandments, Matthew 19:18, Romans 13:9.

B) "The sermon on the mount rewards," Matthew 5:3-12.

"For I was hungry and you gave Me food; I was thirsty and you gave Me drink; I was a stranger and you took Me in; I was naked and you clothed Me; I was sick and you visited Me; I was in prison and you came to Me; inasmuch as you did it to one of the least of these My brethren, you did it to Me," Matthew 25:35-36;40.

C) The Lord's Prayer, Matthew 6:9, Psalm 23, "Exceeding the righteousness of the scribes and pharisee's to enter Heaven with the depth of an un-indictable spirit man," no longer a private hypocrite and public pretender. Matthew 5:20, 1 Timothy 3:1, Titus 1.

D) "Enter through the straight gate, because straight and narrow leads to Life," Matthew 7:13-14.

E) The totality of the fruits of the spirit with faith, hope and charity, Galatians 5:22-23, 1 Corinthians 13:4-13, absent from deviating the Word of God's permissive contextual parameters that justify the statutory motive and intents of God ordained, delegated power within the scope, realm and domain of colored authority, with contrast between the two primary types of mission statement vocation's standard fishing methodologies of bait, mark and netting for fruitful evidentiary substance, empowering either the "man of war policing investigative revenger's material wrath distinctions" from the "clergy's spiritual edifying that prognosticates a pre-emption protectorate from personal liability through the accountability mechanisms of self examination auditing for a lawful living epistle distinction," absent from words or combinations of words that by their very utterance inflict injury, differentiating the spiritual theological infusion for the context centered rules of material reality's mission statement orientation distinction's by either the priestly edification's evangelistic mandate to bait, mark and net for adherency's protectorate from wrath to self, or the same purposed depth of the theological character administration from the statutory authority of verbalized rhetorically pronounced hypothesizing minister revenger's policing investigation activity designs of perceptual transient reproach contained within the investigator's "free-lancing" creativity zone as a methodology of the ensign's standard hostage negotiator actor's fishing reel of psychological appeals and promptings to bait, mark and net the unclean spirit driven criminal presentation into the swat team member's use of force policy wrath zone to stop the threat against persons or property; including psychological warfare verbiage counteracting, that is offering little opportunity for response by crafted aspersions that do not appeal to rational faculties because of the police shielded heretical reverse osmosis mirror, that is illuminating the morbid adversary's reflected countenance by intentionally provoking it's criminal indignation with unessential or gratuitous parts of any exposition of fact or opinion. For out of the abundance of the heart the mouth speaks and can defile the speaker.

"For by your words you shall be justified and by your words you shall be condemned," Matthew 12:37; 13:47-48.

Therefore, the mission statement vocational purpose of police investigative colored authority is overtly clothed as a degree and facet of the Holy Spirit's objective scientific empirical formulas and equations, contextually transposed and personified as a tree known by it's fruit pertaining to a war-zone that is a theologically justified theorized measurement and balanced approach by the pre-eminence of the Bible's water turned into wine wrath distinction by a lawful statutory authority linked to the spiritual calibration of the motive and intent's counteracting against the unclean spirit driven criminal presentation by the minister revenger's complexity formulating methodologies, including the ensign's standard probable cause exigency of verbalized hypothesized voice inflected rhetorical soliloquey's peace officer empowered hostage negotiator actor and it's SWAT team member's use of force policy zone, Exodus 21:13.

F) "If you be led of the Spirit, you are not under the Law's wrath," Galations 5:18.

"The one who offers thanksgiving as his sacrifice glorifies me; to one who orders his way uprightly I will show the salvation of God!" Psalm 50:23.

Wisdom, righteousness, sanctification, redemption, 1 Corinthians 1:30.

Also, historical foundational, timeline understanding of the birth of sin and temptation:

Only one element of material bad fruit in the Garden of Eden, taken and eaten by the woman in collusion with the fruit of bad influence by the devil, caused enmity and death for both parties, Genesis 3:15, opposed to "the Trinity of intellect, power and creation," Romans 1:20.

Application: Sin, satan, self vs. Jesus Christ standards,

Ephesians 2:1-3= The whole warfare theme of understanding the scriptures, from the prophetic Old Covenant to the New Covenant.

"The Lord will send on you cursing, confusion and rebuke in all that you set your hand to do, until you are destroyed and until you perish quickly because of the wickedness of your doings in which you have forsaken Me," Deuteronomy 28:20.

A prioritized focus of mysterious theological theory for preaching with five words, rather than ten thousand words that are confused noise, 1 Corinthians 14:19, or garments soaked in defiled blood, Romans 13:2. Therefore, the "world" is a symbol for the elements of sin, satan, and unregenerate self, of which microscopic parasites are individually and personally obliterated from the mind and it's vision through ascertaining the "end of the Law for Righteousness" by the freewill application exercising of the reciprocating believer "working out their own salvation with fear and trembling," Philippians 2:12, Hebrews 9:26, 1 John 2:15-17; 5:5.

POINT FOUR: THE TRIPARTITE'S EXEMPLARY INDUSTRY, V.61:4

Sub-point: "Glorified" from mastery, Romans 8:30.

Illustrate: The parable of the talents: Matthew 25:14 -30 The reciprocity investments of several-ability literacy with talent, character, position, finances.

"It is required of stewards, they be found faithful," 1 Corinthians 4:2, Acts 5:10.

Application: Perfecting the mastery of competence,

ethical and moral behavior, through disposition, demeanor, lifestyle and postured protocol as blamelessly irreproachable in all respects of personal salvation and living epistle influence of evangelism's "delegated mission statement oriented parameters by the theological pre-eminence formulations from the whole counsel of God" through vocation John 1:14, 1 Timothy 4:16, Romans 12:11, 1 Corinthians 8:10; 10:29.

"As vinegar to the teeth, as smoke to the eyes, so also is the sluggard to them that send him," Proverbs 10:26.

CONCLUSION

A direct appeal too the rationale and reasoning of the free-will's intellectual conscience receptor infused with intuitive sensory perception relating to authoritative sources, objective scientific empirical data transposition of mere inferential subjectivity through summation of the main points by contrasting irrational objections and their associated omission resulting commission type of commensurating liability penalties with the feasibility of perpetuity rewards. "For the Kingdom of God is not eating and drinking, but righteousness and peace and joy in the Holy Spirit. For he who serves Christ in these things is acceptable to God and approved by men," Romans 14:17-18.

Summary of benefits:

"Bless the Lord, O my soul; And all that is within me, bless His holy name! Bless the Lord, O my soul, And forget not all His benefits; Who forgives all your iniquities, Who heals all your diseases, Who redeems your life from destruction, Who crowns you with lovingkindness and tender mercies, Who satisfies your mouth with good things, So that your youth is renewed like the eagle's." Psalm 103:1-5.

A) The conscience protectorate by preeminence and perfection:

"For if we sin willfully after we have received the knowledge of the truth, there no longer remains a sacrifice for sins," Hebrews 10:26.

"For I say to you that this which is written must still be accomplished in Me: And He was numbered with the transgressors. For the things concerning Me have an end," Luke 22:37.

"For Christ is the end of the law for righteousness to everyone who believes," Romans 10:4.

"You shall be hated for My name sake, but he that endureth to the end, shall be saved," Matthew 10:22.

"Who will also confirm you to the end that you may be blameless in the day of the Lord," 1 Corinthians 1:8.

"And he who overcomes, and keeps My works until the end, to him I will give power over the nations," Revelation 2:26.

A Sound Mind and Heart, Hebrews 10:22.

B) Protectorate against all forms of wrath:
John 3:18, Romans 13:5.

"Behold, I give you the authority to trample on serpents and scorpions, and over all the power of the enemy, and nothing shall by any means hurt you," Luke 10:19.

A Peace that passes All Understanding, Philippians 4:7. "Measure the Perfect man, and behold the upright, for the end of that man is Peace," Psalm 37:37.

"Justification by Faith causes Peace with God," Romans 5:1

"Being now Justified by His blood, we shall be saved from wrath through Him," Romans 5:9.

C) 100 fold inheritance and return:

The reciprocity investments from Theological Covenant definitions of character perfection and support of the priestly pre-eminence through stewardship and vocation, wholly sanctified with the tithe or tenth of "seed time and harvest's" business ventures from all contexts of life, Genesis 17:1-2, Genesis 8:22, Exodus 25:3-9, Leviticus 27:30-32, Deuteronomy 28:8, Proverbs 3:9-10, Malachi 3:10, Matthew 6:33; 19:29; 24:47, Acts 5:1-11, 2 Corinthians 1:20.

Perfected leadership for the delegated partnering privilege of governing, ownership and management over all the earth and the substance therein, cultivating blessing, abundance and multiplication lacking in nothing by becoming a "sinless-heat resisting vessel type crucible," burning for the Holy Spirit's internal mechanisms and attributes, from that Holy type furnance vessel, of which refiner's fire purges and tries for a subsequent production and reproduction perfecting from a dross' image and foundation for Christ's, gold, silver and precious stones, (metaphor for the vicarious righteousness from the unblemished, spotless blood atonement as the material support's starting point), Exodus 25:3-9, rather than wood, hay, or stubble, that when crushed by the pestle and tried by fire, doesn't remain, Genesis 1:28-30, Exodus 15:7, Psalm 8:4-8, Proverbs 27:21-22, Haggai 2:8, Malachi 3:3, 4:1, 1 Corinthians 3:12-14. Matthew 5:48; 24:45-47, Luke 19:16-19, 22:36, Hebrews 1:7; 2:7, 1 Peter 1:18-19, Revelation 3:18.

"Kings and Priests that reign upon the Earth," Revelation 5:10.

"And you shall remember the Lord your God, for it is He who gives you power to get wealth, that He may establish His covenant which He swore to your fathers, as it is this day," Deuteronomy 8:18.

"By humility and the fear of the Lord is riches, honor and life," Proverbs 10:15-16; 22:4.

"A doer of the Word," Philippians 4:9.

"A hearer of the Word isn't justified, but the doer of the Word is justified," Romans 2:13, and is likened unto a "wise master builder," whose integrity of foundation and structure can withstand the test and scrutiny of storms, Matthew 7:24.

"Faith without works is dead, and by works faith was made perfect. You see then that a man is justified by works, and not by faith only," James 2:20-24.

Vicarious representation for a conscience reconciliation transposition from wrath and offense for a blamelessly irreproachable God likeness personification presentation of the ambassador's competence, mastery and perfection's glorified justification, evidenced by the sustaining sanctified fruitfulness of it's consecrated promotional influence of wisdom's riches, honor and life. "And Moses said to the people, Do not fear; for God has come to prove you, and that His fear may be before you, so that you may not sin and be faultless," Exodus 20:20, 1 Thessalonians 3:13.

"Do the work of an Evangelist, and make full proof of your Ministry," 2 Timothy 4:5; "Pleading in Christ's stead as ambassadors of reconciliation," 2 Corinthians 5:20.

"Examine yourselves as to whether you are in the faith, prove yourselves. Do you not know yourselves, that Jesus Christ is in you?-unless indeed you are disqualified," 2 Corinthians 13:5.

"Let every man Prove his own work, so that he may have rejoicing in himself alone, and not in another," Galatians 6:4.

"Or, who goeth to war without authority, wise counsel and strategy?" Proverbs 24:6.

"The Lord is a Man of War, and the Lord is His name," Exodus 15:3. Let us pray for: "The Great Commission" to be fulfilled.

"And Jesus came and spoke to them, saying, All authority has been given to Me in heaven and on earth. Go therefore and make disciples of all nations, baptizing them in the name of the Father and of the Son and of the Holy Spirit, teaching them to observe all things that I have commanded you; and lo, I am with you always, even to the end of the age." Amen, Matthew 28:18-20.

"For I testify to everyone who hears the words of the prophecy of this book; If anyone adds to these things, God will add to him the plagues that are written in this book; and if anyone takes away from the words of the book of this prophecy, God shall take away his part from the Book of Life, from the holy city, and from the things which are written in this book," Revelation 22:18-19.

"If we, or an angel from heaven preach any other gospel than, Justification by perfected Faith alone, let him be accursed," Galations 1:8.

Alleluia...

REFERENCES

1) Three versions of the Holy Bible.

2) The General Council of the Assemblies of God standard requirement of 33 college courses for ordination in 2002.

3) The 2005 California Penal Code.

4) Correctional Peace Officer ethics.

5) California Department of Justice, 1990 Post 832 pc powers of arrest manuel.

6) California Department of Justice, 1990 Post 832 pc firearms manuel.

7) California Board of Corrections, 6035 standards and training manuel.

8) Webster's American English Dictionary.

9) October 12, 1988 NSA video proof of Michael Dean Sweetser's challenge, promise and delivery resurrection world record,

substantiated by a CIA witness list of top officials from the United States Judicial, Legislative and Executive branches' of government, including middle eastern Kings.

The aforementioned appraisal of the Holy Bible gets an A+ rating based upon it's immutable infallibility as an authoritative source, evidenced by it's creative design and adherency that is derived from objective scientific empirical data, and substantiated by historical and present day material witnesses' miracle testimonies.

This book capsulates the entire Holy Bible into one expository sermon, synthesizing it's theological theory, by expounding the principles and concepts of legal contract interpretation and application's transposition of the inferential aberration of political subjectivity.

Michael Dean Sweetser, Ph.D. Pastoral Theology.

Printed in the United States
By Bookmasters